AF412867

PELÉ
The King of Soccer

PELÉ
The King of Soccer

Clare and Frank Gault

WALKER AND COMPANY

New York

Photo Credits

The New York Times/Barton Silverman: front cover, back cover, 32;
Wide World Photos: 8, 33-35;   United Press International Photo:
36-42

Our special thanks to Lawrence Reis.

First published in the United States of America in 1975
by the Walker Publishing Company, Inc.

Published simultaneously in Canada
by Fitzhenry & Whiteside, Limited, Toronto.

ISBN: 0-8027-6240-9

Library of Congress Catalog Card Number: 75: 27119

Printed in the United States of America.

10 9 8 7 6 5 4 3 2 1

*For all the thousands
of boys who have played soccer in the
United States, not because it was popular, but because they loved the game.*

A note from the authors

Soccer is the most popular game in the world. In every large country, with the exception of the United States, soccer is king.

In Europe, in Asia, in South America, interest in soccer runs to a high fever. Crowds of 100,000 and more are common. Maracana Stadium in Rio de Janeiro holds over 200,000.

Some stadiums have moats, ditches filled with water, that separate the seat sections from the playing field, to keep the crowd from boiling over into the game. A victory in an important game can set off a city- or country-wide celebration lasting for days. A defeat can drape an entire nation in black mourning.

And seated on the throne atop this most popular sport for the past twenty years has been a small black man from Brazil—Pelé. In all probability, Pelé has been the most popular player who has ever lived, cheered by millions and honored by royalty, presidents, and popes, hailed as "the king of soccer."

Clare and Frank Gault

A small black boy danced barefoot out into the street and began kicking at the air as if he were kicking a soccer ball. But there was no ball. A group of men and boys huddled around a radio nearby. The radio was telling the play-by-play story of a soccer game. It was a local game, Bauru against São Carlos, a neighboring town in southeastern Brazil. The year was 1948.

One of the men smiled as he watched the boy acting like a real soccer player. The boy was about eight years old. His name was Edson Arantes Do Nacimento. Such a big name for a small boy. His friends called him

"Pelé" (pronounced PAY-lay).

Pelé kept kicking at the air as the radio announcer told about the game. Pelé could imagine himself out on the soccer field dribbling the ball downfield with his feet, passing it to a teammate, then taking a pass in return and kicking a goal.

Suddenly, the radio announcer became excited. Bauru had the ball near the São Carlos goal in a good spot to score. Pelé stopped to listen. A player nicknamed "Dondinho" had the ball. He was moving in to take a shot. It looked as if he would score. Dondinho kicked. But he missed. Everybody groaned.

"Bah," one of the men on the street said. "That bum, Dondinho. He's a peg leg."

Pelé jumped as if he had been hit. In a flash, he picked up a brick lying at the side of the street and ran up to the man. His eyes were angry. "Dondinho is my father. You take back what you just said."

The man sneered at Pelé. "Get away from here, you little squirt, or I'll slap your fanny."

Pelé made himself as tall as he could. "You'll fight me, if you are a man."

"Leave the boy alone," said another man. "He's right. Dondinho was the greatest player around here until he hurt his leg. And he's still better than most."

The first man spat on the ground. "Dondinho has always been a bum."

"What a liar you are," the second man said. "Dondinho was a star. You insult our whole team." He gave the other man a push.

The first man pushed him back. And suddenly they were punching at each other. The rest of the group quickly took sides. Soon it was a free-for-all, men and boys pushing and punching each other.

Then Pelé heard a police whistle. Somebody had called the police. "I'd better get out of here," Pelé said to himself. "Papa will be mad if his friends catch me in this." Pelé's father, Dondinho, was one of the policemen in town. He played soccer part time for the local club to earn a little extra money for his family.

Pelé got away and ran home. Soon his father arrived. Dondinho was very sad.

Pelé's mother said, "See what that game does to you. You miss a goal and now you'll be sad for days. I pray Pelé never plays soccer."

Pelé said, "No, Mama, when I grow up I'm going to be a great soccer player, like Papa."

Dondinho smiled and felt better. He knew that Pelé was proud of him no matter what happened. "That's my boy, Pelé."

Pelé's mother frowned. "You're putting too many ideas into the boy's head. Don't blame me for what happens. That game brings nothing but suffering."

That night Pelé's father, mother, grandmother, younger brother and sister gathered for prayers as they always did before going to bed. Pelé prayed he would become a great soccer player. But he knew his mother was praying that he would become an airplane pilot instead.

The next morning, Pelé dressed to go to school. He put on his white shirt with the school emblem and his blue short pants. He put his lunch in a paper bag. He put in his soccer ball, too. Pelé's soccer ball was not a real one. It was one of his father's old socks stuffed hard with newspapers and laced shut with string. It was no bigger than a large orange, and not very round, but it was the only soccer ball Pelé had. He had no money to buy a real one.

Pelé took his little soccer ball everywhere. He would practice kicking it as he walked down the street. He would dribble it. Or aim it at a telephone pole. Or even see if he could pop it into a trash can. He got so he could do almost anything with it.

That morning Pelé left the house, but he didn't plan on going to school. Instead he went to the field behind the town's soccer stadium. He could often get in on a soccer game there. Sure enough, a bunch of boys were ready to play.

The field was just an open patch, flat but rough. It had clumps of grass here and there, but mostly it was dry and dusty. The field had no soccer goals, so the boys who wore shoes took them off and used them to mark where the goals were. Then everybody played barefoot. They had to be careful, though, because Pelé's little soccer ball was hard. One could easily hurt a toe kicking it. They learned to move the ball with the sides of their feet.

Pelé played soccer most of the day with his friends. When he got home he quickly hid his soccer ball, but he couldn't hide all the dirt on his white shirt. His mother knew right away what he had been doing. She grabbed him by the ear and dragged him over her knee to spank him. "Playing hooky from school to play soccer, I'll teach you."

Pelé was spanked often, but it didn't stop him from playing soccer. He joined in these pick-up games at the field as often as he could. The games were fun, but after a while Pelé felt he was missing something. He wanted his own soccer team that could play other teams on a regular soccer field with a real ball.

"If we had uniforms," he told his friends, "other teams would play us as a team. We could call ourselves the 'Seventh of September.'" This is Brazil's Independence Day.

"How are we going to do that?" one of Pelé's friends asked. "We have no money for uniforms. And we have no soccer ball."

"We can earn money by collecting old bottles and junk," Pelé answered. "And we can get a soccer ball by collecting stamps." A candy company was boosting sales of their candy and chewing gum by putting stamps inside all their packages. The stamps had pictures of famous soccer players on them and Pelé had a book to paste them in. When the book was filled, one could get a soccer ball from the candy company.

Pelé and his friends had trouble, though. The stamps had to match certain spaces in the book. Some stamps were easy to get; others were very rare. It took weeks and weeks of watching, trading and begging before they could get the book filled. But finally they did and Pelé sent away for their soccer ball.

While they were collecting the stamps, Pelé became troubled. He went to his father. "Papa, we're collecting stamps with pictures of great soccer players on them. Why isn't your picture on one of them?"

"Oh, Pelé," his father said. "These are the famous soccer players from the big teams in São Paulo and Rio de Janeiro. Bauru is just a little team. I almost had a chance to play for one of the big teams once. Then I hurt my leg and that was the end of it. It's not enough to play the game and work hard, Pelé. You need a little luck, too."

To get money for uniforms, the boys went out to collect old bottles and anything else they could find. They went up and down the streets and alleys. They poked into trash cans. They raked the city dump. Finally, they had a big pile of old bottles, scrap metal, pieces of pipe and old pieces of furniture. They took it all to a junk man to sell. But all they got for their pile of junk was a few coins.

"We'll never make it this way," Pelé said. The future of the Seventh of September team looked dark.

Then Joe, one of the boys, got an idea. "We can make money selling peanuts. We can sell them at the movies, at the circus, everywhere."

"But where are we going to get money to buy peanuts?" asked Pelé.

Joe said, "We don't need money. We can get peanuts from boxcars at the railroad." Many coffee growers in the area were growing peanuts, too, and large shipments of peanuts went through Bauru.

Pelé was surprised. "You mean steal them?"

"What's the difference?" Joe said. "There are tons and tons of peanuts there. All we want are a few."

"What if they catch us?" Pelé asked.

"They won't catch us. First we look. If no one is around, we cut the bags of peanuts with a pen knife. When the bags are cut, peanuts will flow like water."

"And what if they do catch us?" asked Oswald, another one of the boys. "They'll only pull our ears. Nobody arrests boys."

It was agreed. Pelé was doubtful, but he went along with the other boys.

Lunch hour seemed to be the best time. The rail yard and station would be empty. The boys drew straws to see who would carry the pen knife, who would hold the wash basin to catch the peanuts, and who would be lookout to warn them if someone came.

Pelé drew the straw for the pen knife. Joe drew the wash basin and Jack, the smallest one, was to be lookout.

The next day, just after noontime, the three boys crept into the rail yard. There were several boxcars. One had its door open. Pelé and the others crawled under a boxcar and looked around. Nobody was there. Pelé could feel his heart pounding. Sweat popped out on his forehead. His hands were wet and cold.

Slowly, the boys slid along the line of cars until they reached the one with its door open. Jack stayed outside to keep watch while Pelé and Joe climbed into the car. They were in luck. The car was filled with big bags of peanuts. Pelé took a deep breath. He opened the pen knife and cut a slit across the bottom of one bag. Joe held the wash basin underneath to catch the peanuts. And out they poured. In no time, the wash basin was full. They stuffed more peanuts into their pockets. Then they ran.

The other boys met them outside the rail yard. "Whew," said Pelé, "I'm glad that's over with. Now we can roast the peanuts and sell them."

That evening Pelé went to church and prayed to Our Lady of Aparecida, patroness of the area. "Please," Pelé prayed, "forgive us for what we did. We're not bad. We're doing this for a good cause. Just let us get our uniforms. I'll never steal anything again."

The peanuts sold very well and for several days the boys went back for more. Then one day, a worker happened to be in the rail yard during lunch hour. He saw Jack, the lookout, and wondered what he was doing there. He decided to find out. Jack saw him coming and whistled. Pelé and Joe jumped out of the boxcar and ran. The worker chased the boys for about half a mile, then gave up.

"That was close," Pelé said. "We were lucky, but that's the end of the peanuts. They'll be watching for us now."

The boys got together and counted all their money. They had enough to buy shirts and pants, but not enough for shoes and socks.

"What shall we do now?" asked Joe.

"We will have shirts and pants," said Pelé, "that's enough uniform. We'll be known as Seventh of September, the barefoot team."

In a few days their soccer ball came. At first, Pelé was unhappy with it. The ball was made of leather, but wasn't quite as big as a regular soccer ball. Still it was a lot better than a sock stuffed with newspapers.

Since he was the one who collected most of the stamps, Pelé made himself the keeper of the ball. He slept with it. He took it with him wherever he went. It gave him a feeling of importance and also gave him more chance to practice.

As soon as their shirts and pants

came, the Seventh of September team began playing other teams with uniforms. They played everybody they could.

One day, Pelé was playing with the soccer ball in front of his house. He juggled it with his feet, bounced it off his head and knees. A crew of street workers was nearby, fixing up the street, filling pot holes and cutting weeds. They were young men, and soccer fans.

One of the men saw Pelé playing tricks with his soccer ball. "Say, young fella, you look like you can handle a ball," he said.

Pelé looked up. "I play with the Seventh of September, the barefoot team," he said proudly.

The man laughed. "I think I've heard of you. You're pretty big in the little leagues."

Pelé sensed that there was a touch of scorn in the man's voice. "Do you and your fellow workers play?"

"Yes, we all play," the man answered.

Pelé said, "Maybe we can have some fun. We could play a game here on the street during your lunch hour."

That sounded like a good idea and Pelé rounded up his friends. During lunch hour they measured off a section of the street and marked where the goals would be. Alongside the street workers, Pelé and his barefoot team looked very small. The men could run faster, too. But in soccer, being able to handle the ball and teamwork in passing matters more. Pelé and his friends made the others look clumsy. They darted in and out, passing the ball back and forth with their bare feet. They were like a bunch of gnats. Pelé scored three goals as his team outplayed the men.

Near the end of the lunch break, Pelé kicked the ball too hard. It sailed and broke the front window on a neighbor's house. That ended the game. The street crew was happy to go back to work. They were good-natured about the game, though, and helped to spread the word about the barefoot team, and especially about one boy who could do amazing things with a soccer ball.

As Pelé grew older, so did the soccer ball. It was used so much the leather cover wore thin. It began to bulge here and there. It no longer rolled or bounced right. Something had to be done.

"Let's steal one from the sports store," Joe said.

"No. No more of that," Pelé said. "We're not going to steal anymore."

"Then how are we going to get a new ball?" asked the boys.

"We could ask friends and neighbors to help us," Oswald suggested.

That seemed like a good idea. Pelé began by asking his mother for help.

"Oh, no," Pelé's mother said. "Haven't I given enough already? Broken windows. Light bulbs. I have no more money for such foolishness."

The other boys had no better luck. All their families were too poor. They had no money for soccer. Friends in the neighborhood were the same. After a week's effort, they collected almost nothing.

Then Pelé got an idea. During games at the local stadium, a soccer ball would get kicked out into the street once in a while. It didn't happen often,

but it did happen. The wall at one end
of the stadium was particularly low.
Maybe they would get lucky.

Pelé started going to every soccer
game to stand outside and hope a
soccer ball would be hit out of the stadium. Unluckily, a group of people
were always there. They came to see
what little action they could from the
outside without paying for a ticket.
One day, a ball did sail over the wall,
but a man saw it coming and caught it.
And days and days went by when no
balls came over the wall. Pelé was
about to give up. Then one day, a ball
came flying over the wall and landed
near him. Pelé didn't stop to pick it up.
Someone might take it from him. He
gave that ball a kick with all his might.
Then he chased it and kicked it again.
He didn't stop kicking it and chasing it
until he was over a half mile away. He

made sure nobody was after him. Finally, Pelé picked up the ball and hugged
it like a dear friend. At last, a real
soccer ball.

Pelé and the Seventh of September
team continued to play. They became
famous in the area. When Pelé was
about eleven years old, the mayor of
Bauru decided to hold a big tournament for all the younger teams. It
was to be held in the city stadium with
professional referees, just as big league
soccer.

Pelé and his friends wanted to enter
the tournament, but they needed new
uniforms. This time, a traveling sales-
man, Joe Milk, came forward to help.
He was a soccer fan and had heard of
the barefoot team. He put up the
money for uniforms, socks and shoes.
However, he asked that the team be

called "Little America" after his favorite big league team, "America," in Rio de Janeiro.

That seemed to be a small price to pay. Besides, the boys were too excited about the tournament to think about a name. As soon as their equipment came, they started to practice. But after only a few minutes they were unhappy. They had never played in shoes before.

"I can't play with these shoes on," Joe said. "They pinch my feet."

Pelé said, "I can't feel the ball. I kick it, but it won't go where I want it."

So they all took off their shoes and went back to playing barefoot.

One of the tournament officials saw them. "Boys, you have to wear shoes in the games, so you might as well get used to them. Without shoes you can't play."

The boys put their shoes back on.

Pelé grew up in the town of Bauru. It is located in southeastern Brazil. The climate there is warm, like the middle of California.

Pelé takes aim and kicks for the goal. A straight soccer kick is one way to score.

way to kick a goal. Pelé's back is to the
he leaps up and kicks the ball over his
ous "bicycle kick."

Pelé scores again. This time he uses his head to but
ball into the goal. Pelé is 5 feet 7 inches tall, but j
up over the taller goalie. In soccer, only the goal
is allowed to use his hands on the ball.

Pelé controls the ball as he moves around a player trying to block him out.

Pelé gets past two other players who find it's hard to box him in.

Getting and keeping control of the ball leads to plenty of tough action.

Pelé likes teaching soccer to kids. Here he is with a group in Bangkok, Thailand.

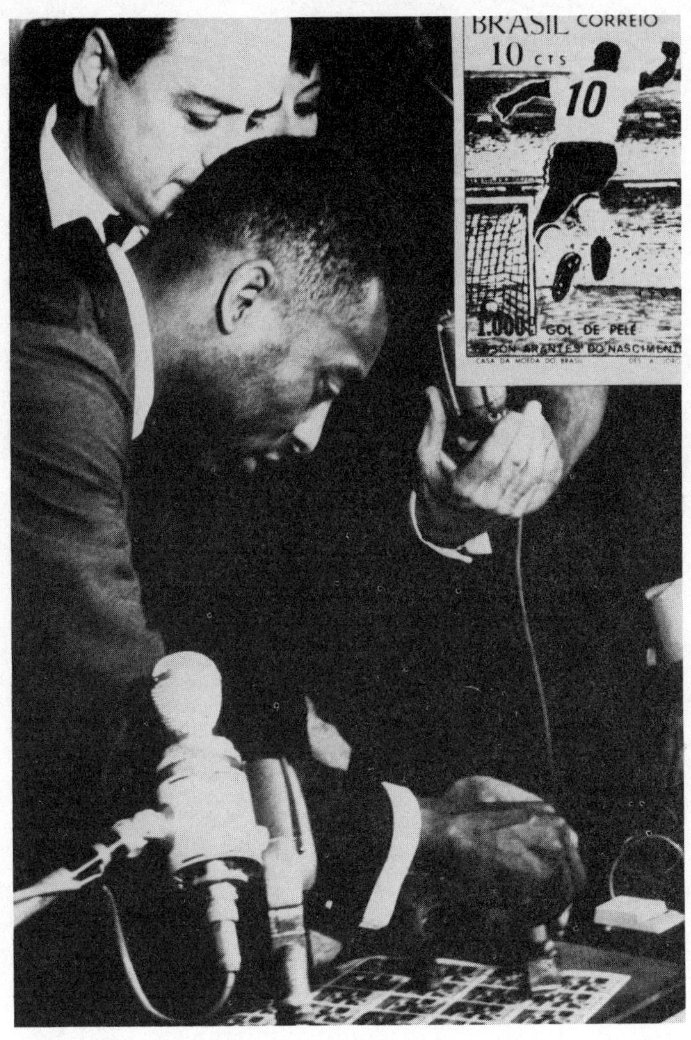

Brazil issued a postage stamp to honor Pelé's 1,000th goal. Pelé pre-cancelled the first ones.

Brazil won the World Cup for the third time in 1970. Pelé made a victory sign during a parade in Paris. (The Arc de Triomphe is in the background.)

In 1975, Pelé came out of retirement after a year. He signed a contract to play for the New York Cosmos. His wife, Rose, was with him.

President Ford tried his foot with a soccer ball. Mr. Ford played football at the University of Michigan. In Brazil, soccer is called "futebol."

They didn't want to, but they had no choice. Three of the boys got blisters the first day. All had sore feet. But they put adhesive tape over the sore spots and bandages on the blisters, and went on practicing.

After a few days, the shoes became more comfortable. And Pelé began to get the "feel" of the ball. He found he could kick with his toes as well as with the sides of his feet. The ball traveled farther with less effort. "Wearing shoes is better," he finally said to himself.

Sixteen teams entered the tournament. Little America won its first game, then went on to play another winner. They won their second game, too, and their third. Suddenly, they were in the finals playing for the championship.

A huge crowd was there. And it was a hard, close game. But years of playing together paid off. Pelé was especially good that day. He was all over the field, dribbling, passing, shooting.

Late in the game, Oswald got control of the ball at midfield. He dribbled it for about 10 yards, then passed it to Joe, who quickly booted it past a guarding player over to Pelé. Another player was in Pelé's way. Pelé dribbled the ball slowly toward the goal. The other player moved in closer to take the ball away. Suddenly, Pelé put on a burst of speed. The other player speeded up, too. Then Pelé stopped cold and changed direction, still keeping control of the ball with his feet. The other player tried to change direction with him, but he slipped and fell to the ground.

In a flash, Pelé was racing for the goal. Only the goalkeeper was in his way now. Out from the net came the goalie to try to smother the ball. Pelé faked a kick. The goalie dove, but the ball wasn't where he thought it would be. Pelé angled a soft shot for the corner of the net. Bounce. Bounce. The goalie raced for it. But it went into the net. It was a goal.

The crowd stood and cheered. In a minute the game ended. Little America had won. The crowd started to chant, "*Pelé, Pelé, Pelé*." Pelé heard his name being called out. He ran around the field, his arms raised in victory. The people threw coins out onto the field. They added up to $3.50, more money than he had ever seen before.

Eleven year-old Pelé was a hero. His father was very proud and talked about him to anyone who would listen. Pelé was feeling pretty good about himself, too.

A few days later, his father came

across Pelé by surprise. Pelé was sitting behind the fence in back of the house. He was thinking about the victory and smoking a cigarette.

His father looked at him for a minute. "How long have you been smoking?"

"Not long," answered Pelé. "Only a few days."

"Do you enjoy it?" his father asked.

"Not really. I just thought I'd try it," Pelé said.

"Well," said his father, "cigarettes will cut down on your wind and nobody needs wind like a soccer player. If you want to be a great player, you'll protect your body." He turned and went back into the house.

Pelé put the cigarette out. He threw the others he had into the trash can. Pelé never smoked again.

The Bauru soccer team got a new

coach. He was Valdemar de Brito. He had been a great soccer player and a member of Brazil's World Cup team. After years of playing soccer, he was now learning to be a coach. He quickly found out that he liked coaching young players best. "It's more fun teaching boys," he told a friend, "You see results. Boys want to learn and will listen to you. Men who have bad playing habits often won't or can't change." He decided to start a junior team in Bauru.

Pelé joined de Brito's team for boys. And his soccer career got a boost. The team had a regular schedule of practices and games. It was run like a professional team.

Valdemar de Brito saw great possibilities in Pelé right away. He spent extra time with him, working on his passing, ball control, and kicking. Pelé was a good pupil. The team was a success, too. They won the local junior championship three years in a row. Pelé was their star.

Pelé's life wasn't all playing soccer, however. His family needed his help. They had little money and everyone who could had to pitch in. For a while, Pelé went to the railroad station to shine shoes for travelers and passersby. He did well enough and was able to add a little to the family fortunes. After that, when he was thirteen years old, he quit school and took a job as a factory hand. He swept floors and helped on the loading dock.

After he had been coaching for three years, Valdemar de Brito quit his job in Bauru. He went to Santos, a large port city near São Paulo, and called on the owners of the Santos team. "There's a great young player in Bauru," he told them. "He's only fifteen years old, but he could play on your first team right now."

The Santos people smiled. They had heard big claims about young players before. "You make too much of this youngster," they said. "How could a boy of fifteen be as good as you say?"

"It's true," de Brito answered. "I've been in soccer all my life and I've never seen ability like this. He could become the greatest player in the world."

The Santos people thought de Brito had gone overboard, but they had to find out. They agreed to give Pelé a tryout with their team.

Valdemar de Brito rushed back to Bauru and told Pelé's parents about his talk with the Santos. Dondinho was excited, but Pelé's mother was against it. "He's just a boy," she said. But Dondinho felt his son should get the chance he himself missed years before. And so it was decided.

His parents bought Pelé some new clothes, including the first long pants he ever had, and sent him off with Valdemar de Brito for his tryout with the Santos. Pelé was nervous. It was the first time he had been away from home. And he wanted his father and coach to be proud of him.

After watching Pelé with a soccer ball for only a few minutes, the Santos people knew they had a good prospect. They put one of their experienced players out on the field to guard him. Pelé dribbled the ball with his right foot as he trotted toward the other player. The other player made a move toward the ball. When he did, Pelé shifted the ball to his left foot, gave him a head and shoulder fake and was past. Pelé made it look easy.

Then they put two players on the field against him. Pelé raced to the right as if he was trying to run around them. The player on that side ran to head him off. Then Pelé quickly shifted the ball and his direction and scooted right between the two guarding players.

Here was a young player of great ability! They signed him to a contract right away. He was to be paid for playing soccer for the first time.

Pelé started with the junior Santos team. He practiced and played with them for three months before he got his first chance to play with the Santos first team. He entered an exhibition game as center forward in the second half and scored his first goal in big league competition. Later that season, he was on the starting team against the Swedish AIK soccer team.

By spring of the following year, Pelé was a regular starter with the Santos. And after only two months of regular play, Pelé became so well known around the big leagues that he was chosen to be on Brazil's national team. He was still only sixteen years old.

In Brazil, as in many countries, there are many fine soccer teams that play each other and also play teams from other countries. But there is also a national team of all-stars that plays other national all-star teams.

In his first game for the national team, Pelé went in during the second half. He scored the only goal for Brazil as they lost to Argentina, 2 to 1. But just a few days later, they played Argentina again. Pelé was a starter and scored another goal. This time Brazil won, 2 to 0.

The next year was a World Cup year.

Every four years the major soccer-playing countries play a series of games ending in a finals to decide the victor. The World Cup is given to the best national team in the world.

Pelé was only seventeen years old, but he was chosen for Brazil's World Cup team. Unluckily, Pelé was injured before the games began. He had a swollen knee and couldn't play in the early games. However, Brazil won without him. But in the quarter finals, against Wales, Pelé was able to start and scored what he feels is one of the most important goals of his career. With his goal, Brazil won 1 to 0, and went into the semi-finals, beating France as Pelé scored three times. And in the finals, Pelé scored twice more as Brazil beat Sweden, 5 to 2.

It was Brazil's first World Cup title.

Pelé had scored six goals in the three games he played.

The next year, Pelé was eighteen years old and had to go into the army. Every boy in Brazil serves a time in the army. Pelé played for the army team, but he also was able to continue playing for the Santos.

Pelé was famous. His feats in the World Cup, with the national team, and with the Santos were the talk of the soccer world. Every team wanted him. Every country wanted him. Large money offers were made to the Santos for Pelé's contract. It looked as if the pressure might become too great to hold him.

Then the government of Brazil acted. Pelé was declared a "national treasure." Brazil had passed a law to stop people from taking national treasures out of the country. The law was meant to protect works of art and important relics. But this time the law was used to keep a human being in the country. All of Brazil knew they had a "treasure" in Pelé and they wanted to hold onto him. After all, Pelé had helped bring them their first World Cup, and they were looking to the future.

And their hopes for the future came true. Brazil won the World Cup again four years later and then again eight years after that. And over this span of years, Pelé's team, the Santos, won state and international team titles time after time. Pelé proved that he truly was a "national treasure."

Pelé scored 1220 goals, including 95 for the Brazilian national team. That is a fantastic total for soccer since many games are low-scoring, often decided by one or two goals.

How could you measure Pelé's feats in soccer in terms of other sports? In baseball, it would be like hitting a home run in every game. In football, scoring a touchdown or two in every game. Or, in basketball, like averaging 50 points per game.

Why has Pelé been such an outstanding player? Speed, of course, is one reason. Pelé can run. And he can change speed quickly. That makes it hard to "cover" him. Other players can't seem to block him out. But his supreme skill is in ball control. Sometimes it almost seems as if the ball were tied to his foot. Other times he seems to have magical control over it. The ball does exactly what he wants it to do.

Imagine that Pelé is dribbling the soccer ball down the field. A player from the other team moves up to block him from going any farther. Suddenly,

Pelé might bounce the ball off the other player's legs, using him as if he were there to help make a bounce pass. Or, Pelé might pass the ball right between the other player's legs, then get control of it again on the other side of him. Or he may pop the ball over the other player's head. There are many ways Pelé can defeat a player guarding him.

Most teams try to stop Pelé by putting two or three players to guard him. Of course, when they do that, Pelé's teammates are in a good spot to score. So Pelé's value to his team is much greater than just the goals he scores. He "sets up" as many goals for his teammates as he scores himself. It's no wonder that Pelé has been acclaimed all over the world as "the greatest soccer player who ever lived."

In 1974, Pelé said he would retire. Giant crowds shouted, *"Pelé, Pelé, Pelé,"* and *"Stay, stay, stay."* But Pelé felt it was time to quit. He was thirty-three years old and probably the richest athlete in the world. He wanted to relax and spend more time with his wife and two young children.

Soccer fans around the world were sad. Brazil acted as if there was a national tragedy. But Pelé was firm. After all, hadn't he faced and beaten every challenge soccer had to offer?

Well, not quite. There was one left. He had tried to ignore it, but after a year of retirement, he couldn't resist trying to beat the last challenge—making soccer a major sport in the United States. For several years, a group of sports people in the United States had been trying to raise soccer in popularity. They had been making progress, but slowly. Several times they asked Pelé if he would help. But every time Pelé said "No." He was tied up with his team and his country. But after a time, Pelé changed his mind. Something should be done for soccer in the United States. He asked for and received the blessings of his countrymen.

In 1975, Pelé signed a contract to play for the New York Cosmos Soccer Team. It was hoped that a player of such fame and ability would excite interest in soccer. And it did. Right from his first appearance, crowds doubled and tripled. There was more interest and enthusiasm in soccer than ever before.

For his efforts, Pelé will receive close to five million dollars which will swell his already large fortune and make him the highest-paid team athlete in the world. But it is the love of the game that brought Pelé to the United States.

Three weeks after arriving in New York, he was seen playing with a bunch of boys in Central Park. It was a pick-up game. When Pelé saw the boys playing he couldn't stay away, just as he couldn't stay from the games when he was only a barefoot kid carrying an old sock stuffed with newspapers.

Pelé's Goals In Major League Games

Year	Number of Goals	Year	Number of Goals
1956	2	1966	42
1957	66	1967	57
1958	87	1968	59
1959	127	1969	68
1960	78	1970	59
1961	110	1971	34
1962	71	1972	50
1963	76	1973	52
1964	60	1974	21
1965	101	Total	1220

Pelé scored 3 goals in a game.....................90 times

Pelé scored 4 goals in a game.....................30 times

Pelé scored 5 goals in a game..................... 6 times

Pelé's Goals—By Team

Santos	1096
Brazilian National Team	95
Army Team	14
Other All-Star Teams	15
Total	1220